Luke and June

Written by Sandra Iversen

Luke is going to use the computer.
He is going to use the computer
to look for monkeys.
Luke thinks monkeys are cute.

June is going to use the computer, too.
She is going to use the computer
to look for dolphins.
June likes dolphins.
She thinks they are cute.

Luke and June
are going to the library.
They are going to use books.
They are going to look
for dolphins and monkeys.

Miss Flute gets the books on monkeys and dolphins for Luke and June.

Luke and June look at the books.
They take notes.

Dolphins

By June Mott

Monkeys

By Luke Hisashi

They make books on dolphins and monkeys.